EXPLORING THE PAST

ANCIENT GREECE

NEIL GRANT
ILLUSTRATED BY YANN LE GOAËC

HAMLYN

Editor: Beryl Creek
Art Director: Gail Rose
Designer: Mei Lim
Picture Researcher: Joanne King
Production: Linda Spillane and Ruth Charlton

First published in Great Britain in 1994 by
Hamlyn Children's Books,
an imprint of Reed Children's Books Limited,
Michelin House, 81 Fulham Road, London SW3 6RB,
and Auckland, Melbourne, Singapore and Toronto.

ISBN 0 600 57122 X

British Library Cataloguing-in-Publication Data.
A catalogue record for this book is available
from the British Library.

Printed in China

CONTENTS

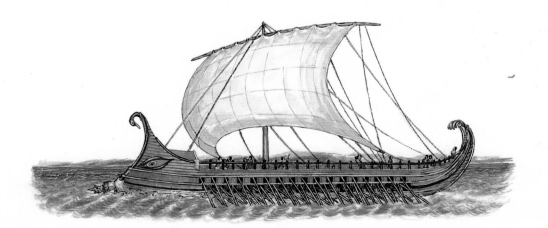

INTRODUCTION

Ancient Greece stands at the beginning of Western civilization. If the Greeks had never existed, the modern world would be entirely different. We cannot measure exactly what we owe to them, but it is easy to make a list of some subjects that the Greeks practically invented. The writing of history itself begins with the Greeks. So does Western philosophy, drama, and most other forms of literature. Nearly all European art has been strongly influenced by Greek art. Mathematics and science really begin with the Greeks.

The Ancient Greeks believed that they were different from other peoples. They

GULF OF TARENTUM

MACEDONIA

Mt. Olympus

THESSALY

Thermopylae

Delphi

ISTHMUS OF CORINTH

Thebes

Marathon

Plataea

SICILY

PELOPONNESE

Athens

Salamis

Piraeus

IONIAN SEA

Mycenae

Olympia

Argos

Epidaurus

Syracuse

Sparta

MEDITERRANEAN SEA

CRET

admired the Egyptians for their wisdom, and the Persians for their laws. They even copied some of their ideas. But they called them "barbarians", which meant "non-Greek". Barbarians might be rich, they might be powerful, they might be just, they might be clever. But they all suffered from one great

disadvantage. They were not Greek!

The Greek attitude to life was different from that of other ancient civilizations where under the rule of godlike kings, everyone lived by the same, unchanging rules. The Greeks had new ideas about what life was about. They introduced reason and humanity to society.

If we could ask the ancient Greeks what was it that made Greeks and barbarians so different, they would probably have replied: "We are free men; the barbarians are slaves."

By that they did not mean only political freedom – that is, the idea that all citizens should have their say in how they were governed. That was an important part of it, but the Greeks' word for freedom meant more. It meant the freedom to think for yourself – the freedom of the human spirit.

Greek civilization can be divided into three "Ages": the Archaic, which lasted from about 700–500 B.C.; the Classical, when Greek civilization reached its peak, from about 500–300 B.C.; finally, the Hellenistic Age, when it spread all over the civilized world and became merged with the civilization of ancient Rome.

Greek civilization did not suddenly appear from nowhere. Besides the older civilizations of the East, the Greeks owed something to their own forbears, the Myceneans, a civilized, Greek-speaking people whose society died out around 1200 B.C. The Myceneans themselves owed something to a still earlier people, the Minoans of Crete. But after the Myceneans, a "dark age" fell upon Greece. Cities disappeared and even the arts of reading and writing were forgotten.

By the time of the great poet-storyteller Homer, in the late 8th century B.C., civilization was reviving. The stories of the Trojan War and the voyage of Odysseus which had been passed down by word of mouth during the dark age, could be written down.

THE GREEKS AT HOME

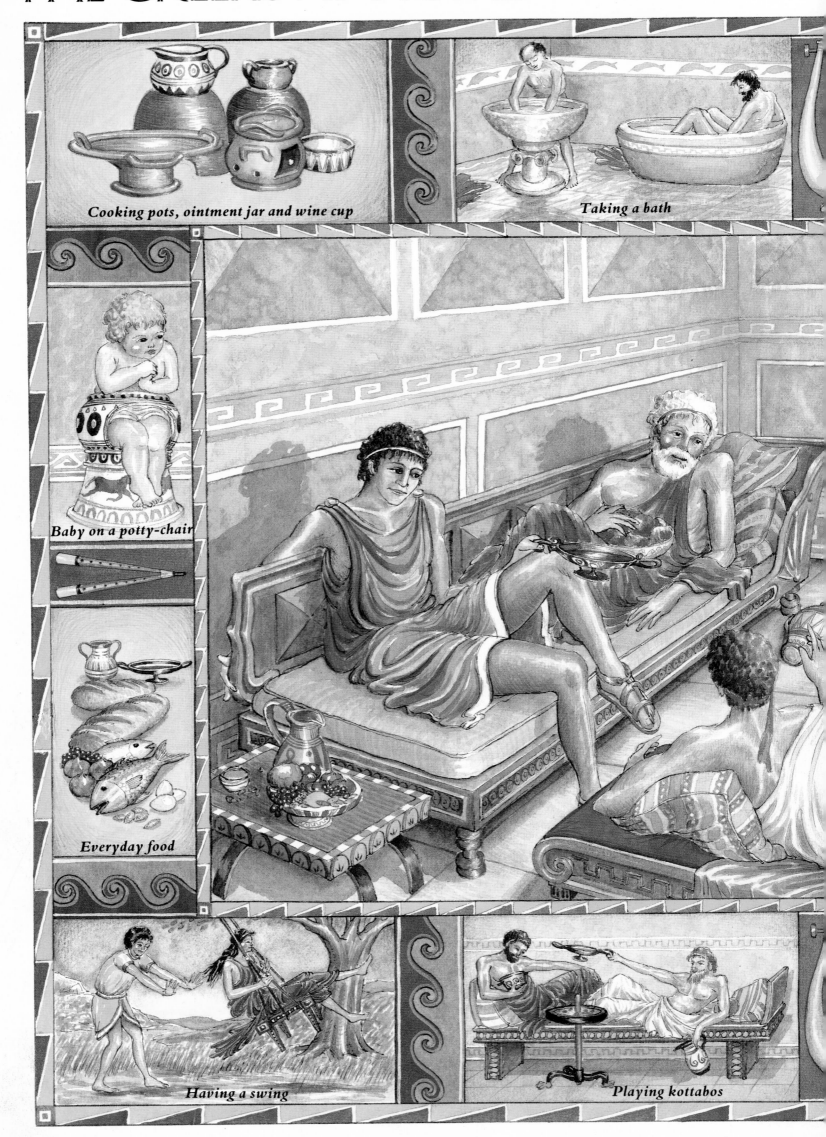

Cooking pots, ointment jar and wine cup

Taking a bath

Baby on a potty-chair

Everyday food

Having a swing

Playing kottabos

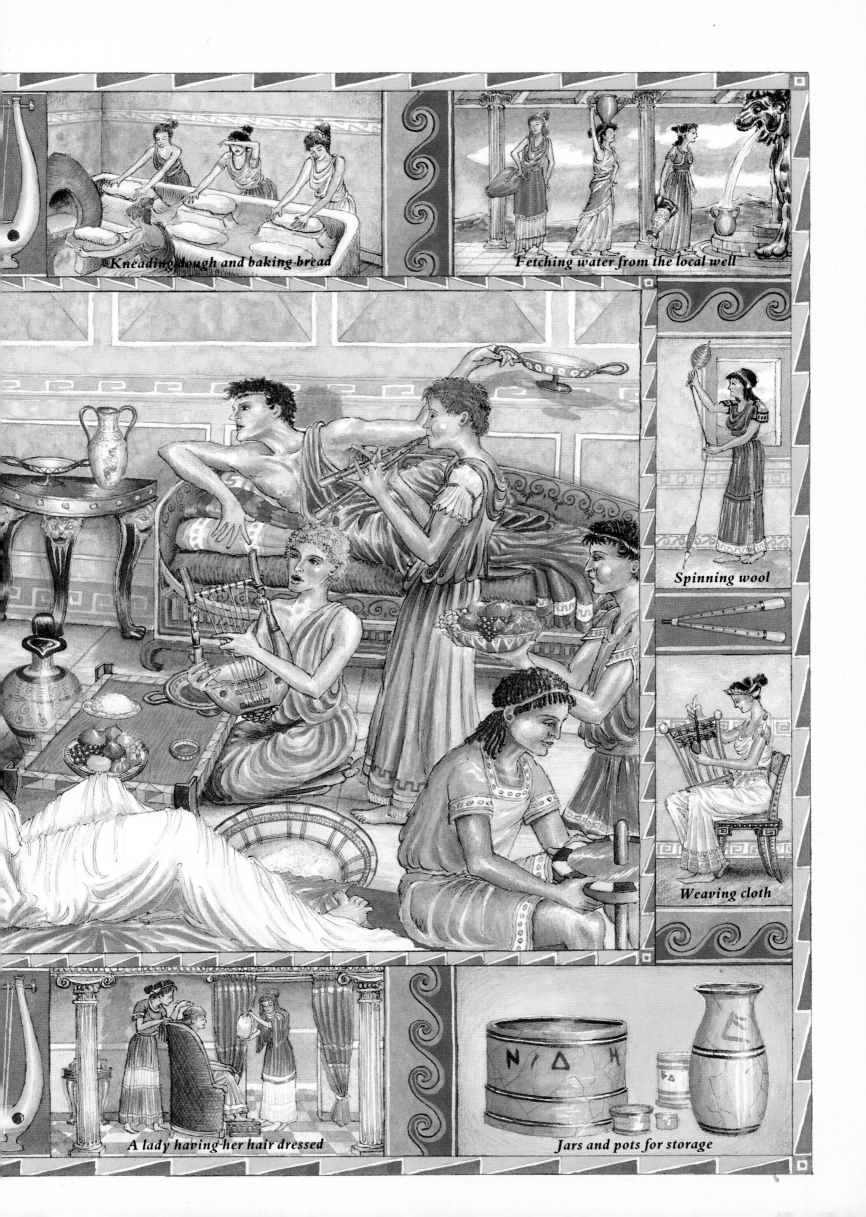

Kneading dough and baking bread

Fetching water from the local well

Spinning wool

Weaving cloth

A lady having her hair dressed

Jars and pots for storage

GOVERNMENTS

All citizens could take part in political debates in Athens, but government was carried on by smaller committees, whose leaders met in the tholos.

The Greeks thought of themselves as one people. They spoke the same language and they shared the same customs. But they were not one nation with one government. They were divided into what we call city-states, and each city-state was independent, although sometimes dominated by a larger neighbour. Wars between them were frequent. The greatest of the city-states (and the greatest rivals) were Athens and Sparta.

Once, the Greeks had been ruled by kings. In the Classical Age, Sparta still had a king (in fact it had two), but apart from the honour, the kings had no actual power except the right to lead the army in war. Otherwise, government was controlled by the citizens, or by a small group of them. In Sparta, a small upper class ruled over a large population of *helots* (serfs, who generally worked on the land), who had very few rights.

In Athens, and in many city-states that were influenced by Athens, much greater freedom existed and government was truly democratic, and free from corruption.

The most important body in Athens was the Assembly, which included *all* citizens: men who had been born in the state. All matters of government policy and law-making were discussed there, and government officials were elected from its members. Poorer citizens, living in farms out in the countryside, probably did not attend very often, and the Assembly could be influenced by a skilful speaker. Still, all citizens enjoyed equal rights, in theory.

However, no government, even of a state as small as Athens, can be run by such a large body of people. Most of the work was done by a council of 500 citizens. They were elected for a year at a time and represented the ten "tribes" or districts into which Athens

A rich man's clothes were richly decorated.

A hoplite – the well-armed foot soldier

was divided. Day-to-day government business was done by a still smaller committee.

The most powerful officials were the ten "generals", elected each year by the Assembly. Their main job was to command the army and navy, but in time they came to be the leaders of the state. Through holding this office, a great leader like Pericles (c.490–429) could become something not far short of a prime minister.

Athenian democracy was more democratic than many modern governments which call themselves democracies, but it had limits. Although all citizens could vote, and become government officials, only about one out of six inhabitants was a citizen.

Women could not vote or become citizens, nor could slaves, nor could the many men living in Athens who were not Athenian-born.

Above left: *Officials and jurors were chosen by lot with the aid of a machine like this. Black and white wax balls were dropped down the tube. If your name was written on a tag opposite a white ball, you were appointed.*

Above right: *Water clocks were used to time the speakers in a debate.*

HOMES AND FAMILIES

The Greeks built magnificent temples and palaces of limestone and marble, but they took less trouble with their own homes. Houses were built of bricks made from mud dried in the sun. Roofs were tiled, and the rooms were built around an open courtyard, with few windows facing out. That made them secure against robbery or attack, but it was also a sign of the importance of the family, or household. Sometimes there was an altar in the courtyard for different household gods.

Some rich families had a fountain in the courtyard, but others had to fetch water in large jars from a public fountain or a stream. The Greeks had no soap and washed themselves in plain water, or by rubbing in

oil or fuller's earth, then scraping it off with a tool called a *strigil*.

In some houses, bedrooms were on an upper floor. Men and women did not mix often. They had separate bedrooms, even if married, and usually ate their meals separately too. Couches were used not only for sleeping, but also eating, although there were chairs (more often stools) as well. Besides three-legged tables and chests for storing clothes, there was little other furniture.

The household was run by the women of the house, helped by slaves. Women looked after the children and did the cooking, except roasting meat which was a man's job (like barbecuing now). They made the clothes,

Plan of a country house. The Greeks did not much care what the house looked like from outside. Security was more important. Even in a city like Athens, with narrow winding streets, houses were usually built round a courtyard, which could not be overlooked.

A family group. Households were larger than modern ones – more children, grandparents and unmarried relatives, as well as slaves.

To our eyes, Greek homes might look plain, even bleak – with little furniture and no soft carpets or cushions. They do not seem to have made much use of cupboards or shelves, but hung objects on hooks on the walls.

starting with raw wool, and baked the bread, starting with grains of corn. There was plenty of work, which was just as well because women did not have much to do otherwise. A woman's place, the Greeks believed, was in the home. Her husband was the boss. She was not a citizen and could not vote. She could not own property of her own. Altogether, women had few rights, even in a democracy like Classical Athens. (In fact, women in Sparta had more rights than in Athens, though otherwise Sparta was a much more conservative place.)

The idea that the sexes are equal would have seemed very strange to the Greeks – women as well as men. So far as we can tell, family life was usually happy, perhaps more often happy (though very different) than family life today. Men respected women as wives, mothers, and as friends, no less than women respected men.

Household slaves had no civil rights, but as a rule they were well treated – no worse (for example) than the servants in a European household in the 19th century.

FOOD AND DRESS

A woman's tunic, or peplos

Himation – *a simple robe*

Chlamys – *a short robe, and a typical broad-brimmed hat*

Because the climate was warm and tastes were simple, the Greeks wore loose, simple clothes usually made of wool. A woman's tunic was little more than a rectangle of cloth, as it came from the loom. No cutting and not much sewing were needed. It was draped around the body, fastened over the shoulders with pins or ribbons, and gathered at the waist by a girdle or belt. The poet Homer often described beautiful women as "white-armed". That was not because their arms were whiter than the rest of them, only that their arms were bare.

Men also wore simple tunics, sometimes ankle-length, sometimes above the knee. Outdoors, a cloak was worn on top. Such clothes, like the belted plaid once worn by Scottish Highlanders, could be arranged in many different ways. A fold could be drawn over the head to form a hood, though men sometimes wore hats of various kinds.

Fashions changed in Greece, though nothing like as fast as they do now. Wealthy Athenians in the 6th century wore richly woven, purple tunics, a fashion influenced by Persia. After the Persian wars, dress became plainer again, and men wore only a simple cloak, called a *himation.*

Rich Greek women wore their hair long, and it was done up in many different styles, sometimes taking hours to arrange. Some dyed their hair or wore wigs, as well as make-up to whiten their faces and darken their eyes.

The Greeks were less ashamed of nakedness than we are. Athletes at the Games, for example, usually wore nothing at all. Indoors, people often went barefoot. Outside, the usual footwear was sandals, sometimes with a thick sole and metal studs. Boots with long pointed toes were sometimes worn.

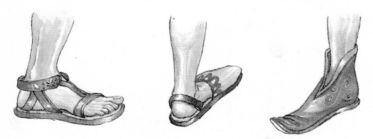

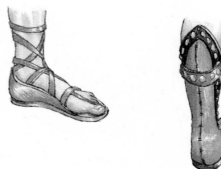

People often went barefoot, but there were sandals, shoes or boots like these.

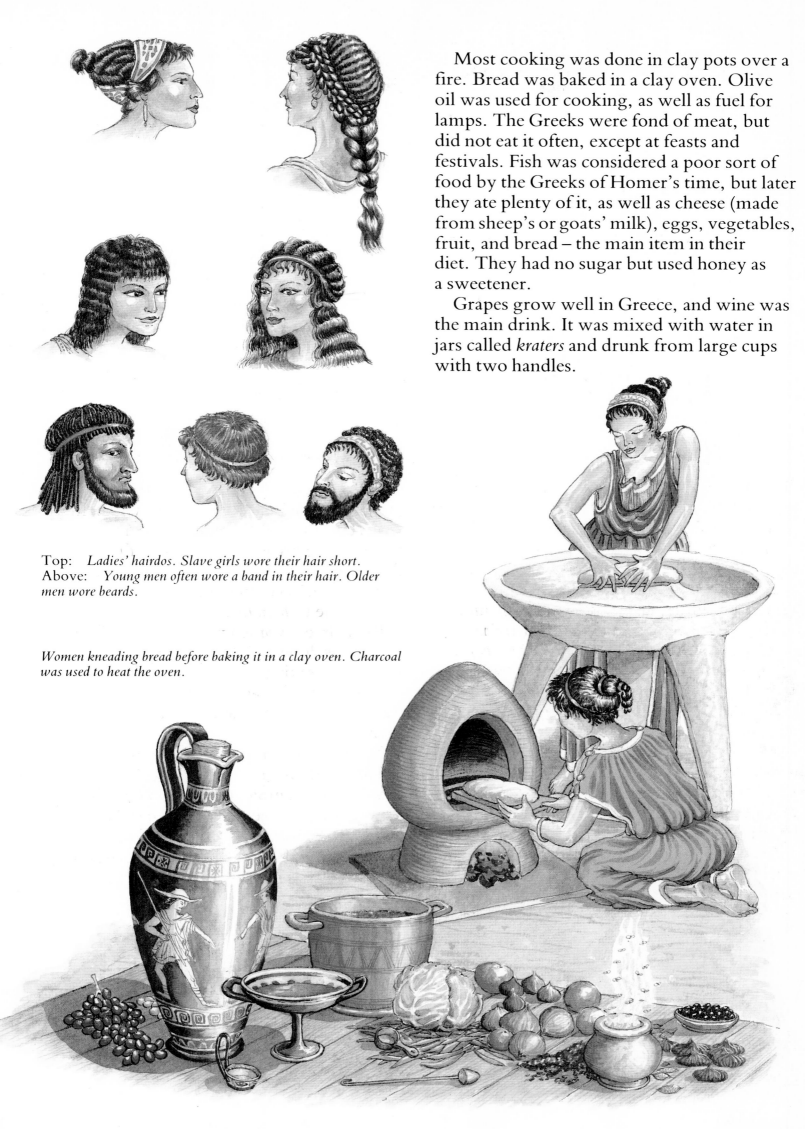

Most cooking was done in clay pots over a fire. Bread was baked in a clay oven. Olive oil was used for cooking, as well as fuel for lamps. The Greeks were fond of meat, but did not eat it often, except at feasts and festivals. Fish was considered a poor sort of food by the Greeks of Homer's time, but later they ate plenty of it, as well as cheese (made from sheep's or goats' milk), eggs, vegetables, fruit, and bread – the main item in their diet. They had no sugar but used honey as a sweetener.

Grapes grow well in Greece, and wine was the main drink. It was mixed with water in jars called *kraters* and drunk from large cups with two handles.

Top: *Ladies' hairdos. Slave girls wore their hair short.*
Above: *Young men often wore a band in their hair. Older men wore beards.*

Women kneading bread before baking it in a clay oven. Charcoal was used to heat the oven.

13

SPORTS AND GAMES

The Greeks lived an outdoor life and believed that games and competitions were healthy. Athletics meetings were held at religious festivals, along with music and drama competitions. The Olympic Games, held every four years, were so important that the Greeks used them as a calendar. The first year in the calendar was our 776 B.C., when (so the Greeks believed) the first Olympic Games had been held.

Other Panhellenic ("all-Greece") games were held in other years, so there was one somewhere each year. Many events, like the discus and the javelin, are the same today. But the first "marathon" was not a race. The name commemorates a messenger who ran non-stop to bring news of the battle of Marathon (a victory over the invading Persians) to Athens in 490.

Successful athletes brought honour to

An athlete binding his hair with a filet, or band, a sign of victory.

themselves and their city, and were treated as heroes – just as they are now. A famous athlete like the wrestler Milon had statues made of him and became as famous as Pelé or Muhammad Ali. Men trained at a public *gymnasium,* which was not a building like a modern gym, but an open space, usually with a stream nearby.

There was nearly always a war going on somewhere in Greece, but during the

One team game was played with a ball and sticks similar to hockey sticks.

The stadium at Olympia, where athletic events took place during the great religious festival. It was designed for foot races and was nearly 200 metres long.

Panhellenic Games, a truce was declared. Although it often did not stop the fighting, it did allow safe passage to athletes travelling to the Games.

The Greeks also played team games, though we do not know the rules, and in quiet times board games like draughts. Rougher sports, like chariot racing or cock-

fighting, were popular with spectators. Children played many games of their own with hoops, carts, balls, and so on. Homer, in the 8th century, described a princess playing ball with her ladies by a stream while waiting for the washing to dry.

There were more wild animals about than there are now – in Homer's time lions may still have lived in northern Greece – and upper-class men showed their skill and bravery in hunting. We are told that Homer's hero, Odysseus, had a scar on his thigh made by a wild boar before he speared it. Hunting also provided extra meat for roasting. Fishing might have helped fill the pot too, but few, if any, adults went fishing for sport. It did not challenge a man's strength and courage as hunting did, and fish were not a noble quarry. In Greek literature, professional fishermen are usually rather poor and wretched fellows.

THE GREEKS AT WORK

Knocking down ripe olives with sticks

A fisherman with his catch

Miners' lamps

Agricultural tools

Shoemaker shaping a piece of leather

Merchant weighing his goods

Putting the finishing touches to a marble urn

Forging tools

Iron tongs

Hammer heads

Pressing juice from grapes to make wine

Prisoners of war working in a mine

FARMING

As in all ancient civilizations, farming was much the most important job and employed most of the people. It was a Greek tradition that free men should own land, and a man's wealth was measured by the amount of land and animals he owned.

Good farm land is scarce in Greece. The soil is mostly poor, and the land is mountainous. As bread was the main food, wheat and other cereals were the main crops, but Athens, for example, could only grow about one-third of the grain it needed. The rest had to be imported from the Black Sea region and other places.

The summer in Greece is hot and dry, so the grain was sown in autumn and reaped in May, before it shrivelled in the heat.

Olives and grapes (harvested in August) were also big crops. The Greeks drank milk and made cheese, but not butter; they used olive oil instead. Grapes were grown to make wine. Vines could be grown on mountain slopes, so they did not take up land needed for grain and other crops. The Greeks also raised vegetables such as beans, peas, lentils, onions, cabbages and lettuce.

Goats were kept for milk, and sheep mainly for wool. They could graze on poor

Farms were small, and few animals were kept. Horses were rare except for the rich. Mules and oxen were used for ploughing.

The Greek plough was a simple machine, little more than a pointed pole tipped with metal, which made a furrow but did not turn the earth over. Wheels were added later.

The seed was sown by hand.

mountain pastures, but good grazing land for cattle or horses was harder to find. The meat most often eaten came from pigs and young goats. Chickens provided eggs, and bees gave honey. Donkeys and mules were kept for transport.

The Greeks did not enjoy working. It was just something that had to be done. If you were rich enough, you did not have to work, and that was fine. The Greeks saw nothing to admire in working for a living.

However, farming was accepted as the most respectable kind of work, and most of the citizens of the Greek states were farmers. Many farms were quite small. They were worked by the farmer with the help of his family and one or two slaves or servants. Much bigger farms also existed, owned by rich landowners who did not have to work themselves. In Sparta, which had the largest area, the land was divided up among the citizens and worked for them by *helots*. As the number of citizens was quite small, a very large estate could be owned by one family. On the plains of Thessaly, which was the one region where cattle could be raised in large numbers, big estates owned by nobles and worked by slaves were the rule.

Grain was harvested with one-handed sickels with iron blades.

The grain was threshed on a round stone floor by oxen or donkeys. The wind carried away the chaff.

WORKERS AND CRAFTSMEN

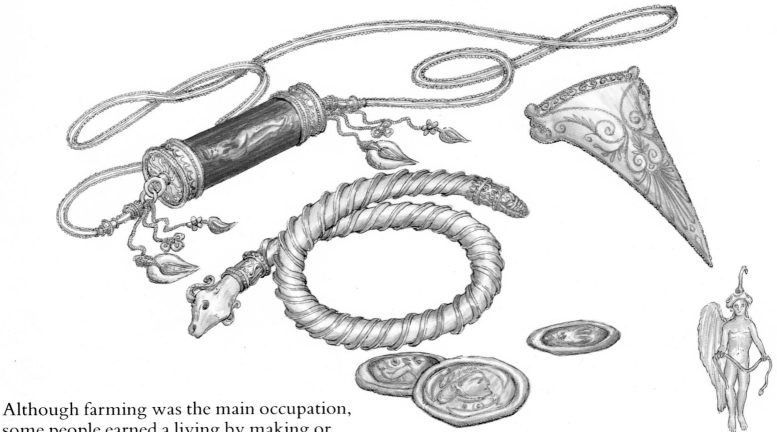

Although farming was the main occupation, some people earned a living by making or selling things. In later times some merchants became rich men, but most craftsmen and traders were not wealthy. Because they were forced to spend most of their time working, more fortunate people looked down on them.

There were no factories in ancient Greece. Objects like shoes or swords or wine jars were made in small workshops, which were run by a family of craftsmen with the help of a few slaves. There was a shield-maker in Athens who employed about a hundred slaves, but that was an unusually large business, due to the big demand for shields during the Peloponnesian War.

The workshops where the goods were both made and sold were often in the front of the family's house, facing the street. They were grouped together in the area of the town called the *agora,* an open space with colonnades around it, which was both a market place and a civic centre with grand public buildings. Here, side by side, were craftsmen making pottery, bronze and iron tools, marble statues, leather, baskets and other goods. Sons learned the trade from their fathers, and the business was passed on in the same family.

The craftsmen who made jewellery, gold and silver and other precious objects were extremely skilled. They had all the techniques, though not the tools, used by craftsmen today.

The largest industries in the Greek world existed outside the cities – in the mines and quarries. Greece was short of metals, but Athens was lucky enough to have silver mines at Laureion (Laurium), which also provided lead. The mines were owned by the government, which let them out to private citizens. The actual work was done by gangs of slaves, as many as 20,000 at one time. Although a slave who worked in a house or a workshop might be well treated, the life of the slaves who worked in the mines was grim and cruel. A man often stayed there until he died. Working on all fours, or lying on his back, in narrow "galleries", he often died rather soon.

Although the Greeks had to import many metals, they had large supplies of marble and limestone for building. The huge stone quarries at Syracuse in Sicily, where thousands of Athenian prisoners of war worked after being captured in 413, still exist today. The historian Thucydides gives a horrifying account of the sufferings of those men, forced to work under a scorching sun surrounded by piles of stinking corpses.

One of the black marks on the history of Classical Greece is the treatment of the slaves who worked in stone quarries and mines. They were often men captured in war. Some of them managed to become rich enough to buy their freedom, but more often their fate was hard labour, suffering and early death.

TRADE AND TRAVELLERS

A Greek merchant was an adventurer. He hired or owned his own ship, and loaded it with goods that were cheap in his home port. Then he sailed to a place where he could sell his cargo at a profit. He sailed from port to port, buying what was cheap and selling what was expensive. Sometimes he exchanged one sort of goods for another, a form of trade called barter. But the Greeks also had money – mostly silver coins. The trouble was that each city-state made its own coins, and their value changed from place to place.

A huge number of products were traded among the Greeks and their neighbours. Food and wine, cloth, and raw materials like timber or metals made up the biggest cargoes. Athens could never grow enough grain to feed its people, so the Athenians had to import corn. But they grew more olives than they needed, so they exported olive oil to other states. The Athenians also exported pottery and other manufactured goods all over Greece, and to neighbouring countries. Other places were famous for special products too – the island of Rhodes for its wine, Cyprus for its almonds.

Because Greece is such a mountainous country, most goods travelled by sea. The mountain passes were too rough for carts,

Silver, gold and bronze coins like these were used all over Greece. The best-known was the "owl" which was issued by Athens. The owl was the symbol of the goddess Athena.

Merchant ships unloading grain, hides and wine (in large jars called amphorae*). Athens imported hundreds of products, from as far away as Egypt and the Black Sea.*

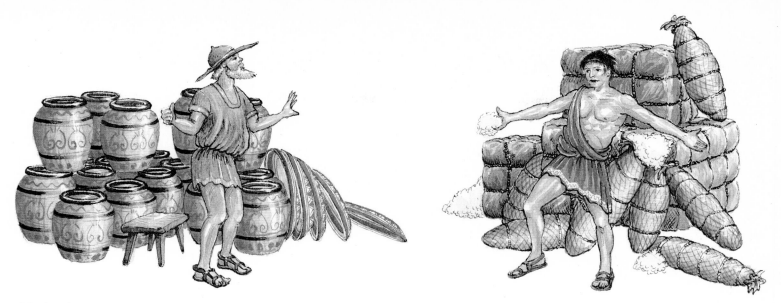

Traders bartering goods. The merchant on the left is trying to exchange his pottery for bales of wool and jars of wine.

and bulky loads could not be carried on the backs of donkeys. Robbers also lurked in the hills.

Even if the goods were going to a town in the next valley, it was easier to ship them up the coast. But the sea was also perilous. The Aegean Sea contained many quiet coves where pirates waited for a merchant ship to pass that way.

In the 5th century, the powerful Athenian navy cleared most of the pirates from the seas, but the danger of shipwreck remained. Although the Mediterranean is usually a calm sea, storms blow up suddenly, and there are many dangerous passages around rocky coasts. Ships stayed close to land, and put in to the beach at night. Summer was the safest season for sailing, and few ships ventured on to the open sea in winter.

In spite of the difficulties, the Greeks enjoyed travelling. They came from all over the country to the Games at Olympia or to the Panathenaic festival at Athens. At other times too, Athens had a large number of "foreigners" living in the city. As there were no hotels, travellers depended on ordinary people for food and shelter. It was a tradition to welcome strangers. A traveller might expect to be given water for washing and food to eat with no questions asked – at least until he had finished eating.

A papyrus document

Child gymnasts

Surgeon's scalpels

Forceps and drill

A physician and a sick boy

Surgeon and patient

Spartan boys were flogged to teach them to bear pain

A writing lesson

Writing equipment

Wax tablet

Gear wheel on windlass

The first steam engine

SCHOOLS AND TEACHERS

Although education was not formal, like ours, teaching was often one-to-one, each boy having his own tutor. A pupil wrote on a wooden board coated with wax, using a pointed instrument called a stylus.

Children were important to their parents partly because they were their investment for the future. There were no pensions, and old people needed children to look after them. Daughters would not inherit property or wealth.

Small children saw more of their grandparents, who were no longer so busy, than they saw of their fathers. Boys were often named after their grandfathers.

But fathers had the power of life or death over their children. In many places, unwanted babies were abandoned, perhaps to die, more often to be found by people who would bring them up, probably as slaves. In Sparta, babies born with a handicap were

usually thrown over a cliff.

There was no education system in ancient Greece. Sons of citizens had their own tutor or "pedagogue", who was usually a household slave. In 5th-century Athens, professional teachers set up their own schools, teaching the sons of rich citizens for a fee. They specialized in four main subjects: reading and writing, music, and athletics. A smaller number of boys went to teachers of rhetoric – the art of public debating – about the age of 15, and perhaps to a famous teacher of philosophy, like Socrates (died 399 B.C.).

As the army was made up of citizens, every citizen had to be trained to fight. Athenian boys spent two years in military service from

Girls in Sparta were trained in athletics.

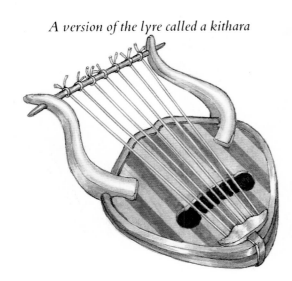

A version of the lyre called a kithara

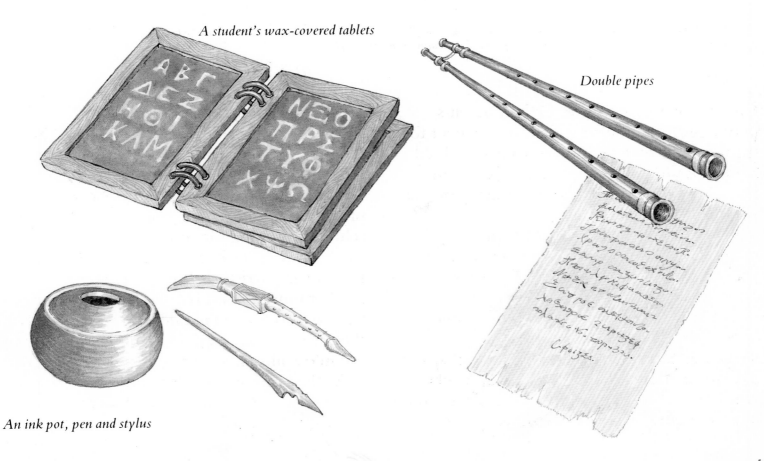

A student's wax-covered tablets

Double pipes

An ink pot, pen and stylus

the age of 18, when they became citizens.

Girls were educated at home, by their mothers and by household slaves. Their chief studies were what we would call home economics, but they probably also learned reading and writing, music, and perhaps other subjects. Reading and writing were less important in ancient Greece, where books were rare, than talking and listening.

In earlier times, education was mainly training for war, and in Classical Sparta it still was. At the age of seven, the sons of Spartan citizens were taken away from home and sent to very tough boarding schools. They were given few clothes and little food, and they were not even allowed beds to sleep in. The music they learned was marches and war songs, their games were weapons drill and battle practice.

At the end of their schooling, they were sent into the country to live as best they could by stealing from the *helots*. They were expected to prove their courage by killing a man. But Sparta was an extreme case.

THOUGHT AND IDEAS

For most ordinary people in ancient Greece, the world was strange and mysterious. Magic and superstition were all around. Even a river or a tree was a kind of spirit. Yet the Greeks learned to see things not as the work of angry gods or supernatural creatures, but in a spirit of reason.

In 357, some Greek soldiers were frightened by an eclipse of the Sun, which to them was a completely mysterious happening. Their general, Dion, reassured them. There was no need to worry, he said, because there was certainly some natural reason for it. It was not a terrible omen. This attitude was new in the world. The Greeks believed that the universe obeys laws, and that those laws could be discovered. They were the first people who tried to find the causes of things by reason, instead of accepting supernatural explanations.

The philosopher Epicurus teaching astronomy. Epicurus, a kind and gentle man, was unusual because he taught young women as well as men. His school met in the garden of his house.

They were able to do this because they were "free men". They could discuss any subject openly, without fearing the anger of some powerful king such as the ruler of Egypt or Persia.

The Greeks had a strong sense of curiosity, and their search for the causes of things marks the beginning of philosophy and science. Like explorers advancing into unknown lands, they opened new areas of the human mind. They were the mental pioneers of Western civilization.

They believed that the truth is always simple. It is just a matter of finding it, and this can be done by reasoning. Socrates tried to find the answers to such difficult questions as "What is 'justice'?" by his method of strict questions and answers. The young, upper-class men of Athens who were his pupils found that every answer they gave only produced another question.

The Greeks produced some of the greatest thinkers the world has known. Men like Plato or Aristotle were just as clever as any person who ever lived, before or since. They were far cleverer than most of us! The difference

Aristotle attended Plato's Academy for 20 years, and later became tutor to Alexander the Great.

between them and us is that we have had over 2,000 years of experience, in which human knowledge has gone on increasing. They started from almost nothing. In spite of that, Aristotle (384–322) was the chief authority on many subjects for nearly 2,000 years after his death, and philosophers today are still arguing over ideas that were first raised by Plato (c. 427–347).

Socrates was the first of the great philosophers of Classical Athens, yet, so far as we know, he never wrote a word. His ideas come to us through the writings of his pupils, especially Plato. In about 387 Plato founded an Academy in Athens, which we may think of as the first university.

SCIENCE

With their lively minds and their sense of curiosity, the Greeks were good at thinking of explanations for things. Their ideas were often completely wrong, because they did not test them, as modern scientists do, by experiments. The Greeks used their eyes and brains to think up theories that were sensible, even if untrue.

For example, most Greeks believed that the Sun moves around the Earth. If you use your eyes, that seems obvious. Yet some people questioned it. In the 3rd century, Aristarchus of Samos suggested that the Earth moves around the Sun – an idea that was not accepted as true for nearly 2,000 years.

The Greeks believed that everything is made up of a small number of elements – fire, air, water and earth. Differences are the result of different mixtures of the elements. Greek philosophers also developed a theory of the atom – that everything is made up of very small particles of matter.

Xenophanes believed that great movements of the land had taken place in the past because he found seashells on mountains.

Euclid, who lived about 300, was the father of mathematics, although he used methods which had come down from Pythagoras, about two centuries earlier. Euclid explained basic ideas in geometry like an angle and a line, which he defined as something that has length but no breadth.

Aristotle was the greatest natural scientist. He believed in collecting as many facts as possible *before* forming a theory, and he was the true founder of biology. He examined how living things were made and worked out a system for classifying plants and animals.

Many of the advances in science and technology took place in the Hellenistic age, especially in the Greek colony of Alexandria. There, Eratosthenes measured the size of the Earth, Archimedes invented his famous screw, and calculated the value of π – the Greek letter used as a symbol for the ratio of the circumference of a circle to its diameter. Ptolemy advanced the study of astronomy and geography.

Euclid working out a problem in geometry.

The first use of a screw was in a kind of pump invented by Archimedes.

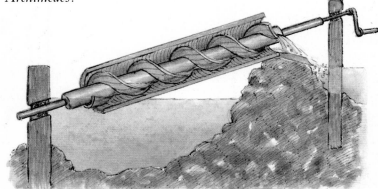

In ancient times, illness was thought to be a punishment from the gods. The Greeks were the first to practise medicine that was scientific, not magical. Hippocrates taught the importance of diagnosis – discovering the nature of the illness. The Hippocratic Oath, which many doctors today know by heart, was a kind of code of practice for doctors.

Greek doctors did not know about germs and infection. They avoided operations if they could, because they were so dangerous (and, with no anaesthetics, painful!). They had no chemical drugs but used many herbal medicines, and they understood the importance of rest and exercise.

A doctor with his patient

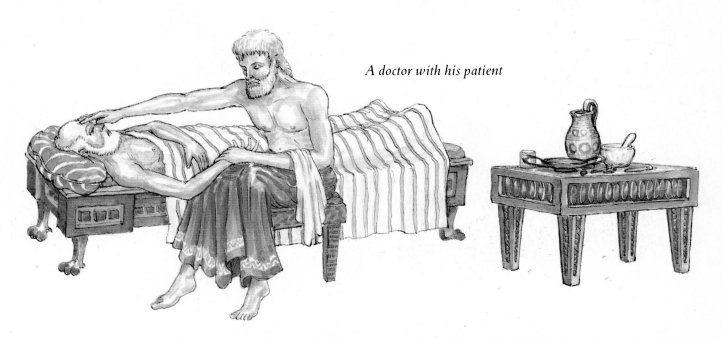

ARTS AND CRAFTS

A lyre and reed pipes

Listening to music

Mask for comedy

Storage jar

A temple site

Painting a vase in a pottery

Actors wearing masks

Doric   Ionic   Corinthian

Mask for tragedy

Wine jug

Sculptor at work

Bronze handle in the shape of a horse

LITERATURE AND MUSIC

The story of European civilization begins with the Greeks and it ends (so far) with us. But in some ways, the Greeks were more "civilized" than we are. Most of our arts and sciences owe something to the Greeks, as well as most forms of literature. The Greeks "invented" many forms of poetry, drama, history and philosophy, and in all those forms Greek writers set the highest standards.

Epic poetry, which is poetry that tells a heroic story, begins with Homer in the 8th century. The two books of Homer, which were probably written down after his death by someone else, are the *Iliad* and the *Odyssey*. The *Iliad* tells the story of the Trojan

War, when the Greeks captured Troy by smuggling soldiers into the city inside a Wooden Horse. The *Odyssey* tells of the adventures of Odysseus, or Ulysses, after the war had ended. These stories, in which gods as well as people play a part, are legends, which had been passed down by word of mouth during the "dark age" of Greece. Yet we now know there *was* a Trojan war, so the legends may have been based on real events.

Homer's poetic stories became almost like holy books to the Greeks. They are also the earliest works of Western literature that we have today. Unfortunately, we know nothing about Homer himself. He may have been not one man but two, or even more.

Homer tells the story of the destruction of Troy in the Iliad.

In Homer's Odyssey*, the hero has himself tied to the mast of his ship so he will not be tempted by the song of the bird-like sirens.*

Greek poetry was not written to be read, but to be heard. It was recited at religious festivals and dinner parties. It was not spoken, but chanted, or sung, often with music and sometimes dancing as well.

The first real novel was not written until the 2nd century A.D., but stories in prose are much older. *Aesop's Fables,* tales of animals which teach a human lesson (like the story of the hare and the tortoise), are as old as the 6th century B.C. Like Homer, Aesop is a mystery. There may have been no such person.

The only "history" which was written before the Greeks was lists of the triumphs of kings. They were written only to glorify the rulers, and were more legend than history. Herodotus, who wrote about the Persian Wars of the Greeks, tried to get the facts from papers and interviews. Thucydides recorded the triumphs and horrors of the Peloponnesian War, between Athens and Sparta and their allies. Both men had taken part in some of the events they described, but they tried to be fair to both sides.

The Greeks liked music with everything. They had special songs for different times, such as work songs, harvest songs, drinking songs and so on.

THEATRE

Greek tragedy grew out of the celebrations at religious festivals. The plays were entered in a competition, with prizes for the winners. The plays of the great tragic dramatists of Classical Athens, Aeschylus, Sophocles and Euripides, were based on well-known myths about the gods and men, so the audience knew the main story already. The actors were all male (like Shakespeare's actors) and they wore masks. Very little action took place in tragic drama, and violent events usually happened off-stage. There were only about three main actors, who might play more than one part, together with a Chorus of singers and dancers. In comedies, the Chorus was sometimes dressed in animal costume, as in Aristophanes's popular play, *The Frogs*.

Tragedies and comedies were performed together, and the audience usually saw three plays at a time. Both tragedies and comedies were in verse, and music and dancing were an important part of all drama.

There was no censorship in ancient Greece, and the comedy of Aristophanes and other writers is often extremely rude, making fun of famous people. Aristophanes, for example, mocked the philosopher Socrates cruelly, although Socrates himself might have been in the audience.

In Greek theatres the audience sat on higher levels than the actors, and there was no raised stage.

The theatre was in the open air, with rows of seats rising in a half circle around the "orchestra", where the performance took place. "Tickets" were bronze discs, bearing a seat number. Theatres were often built on the side of a hill, to make construction easier. The orchestra was a circular floor paved with stone, very like the threshing floor on a farm. At the back was a low wooden building with a large central doorway. This was the only "set", and it was not changed during the play. It could stand for a palace, a temple, a city wall, and so on. Otherwise, not much scenery was used, and of course there was no curtain. But plays did make use of some stage machinery. Actors could be raised in the air by a kind of crane, or moved through the central doors at the back on a low platform on wheels.

Greek drama belongs chiefly to one place and one time. All the great dramatists were Athenians, and they all lived within a few years of each other. Soon, drama festivals and theatres spread all over the Greek world. Later, they were created in the new cities in the east founded by Alexander the Great. But by the 4th century, the great age of Greek drama was over. The old plays were still performed, but later playwrights never reached the same high peak of poetic drama.

A "ticket" for the theatre.

Actors in comedies and "satyr plays" (a kind of farce) wore comic, padded clothing and fantastic masks.

37

ARCHITECTURE

The temples, which the Greeks built as homes for their gods and goddesses, were the greatest monuments of their civilization. Some can still be seen today.

Architects at work today may be called "modernists" or "classicists". A "classical" building is one which is designed in the tradition that began in Classical Greece.

The Greeks were limited by the materials and the building methods that were available. In spite of those limits, they created buildings, like the Parthenon in Athens, which are as perfect as a building can be.

The main building material was stone. For really grand buildings, it was marble, but more often it was limestone, which was cheaper and easier to work. The stone was cut into blocks the right shape and lifted into position by ropes and pulleys. Although metal dowels or wooden pins helped to stop the blocks moving, the buildings were held together by weight, as the Greeks had no mortar or cement.

For the same reason, the Greeks seldom built arches or domes. Their architecture was one of straight lines, and their buildings were bold and simple (though not so simple as they

look). Great care was taken in planning, and Greek architects made the best possible use of angles, proportions and views.

Nearly all great public buildings had a row of columns across the front, and the triangle of space between the capitals of the columns and the peak of the roof was often decorated with sculpture.

There were two styles, or "orders" for these colonnaded buildings. In most of mainland Greece, the order was Doric, named after the Dorian race who had settled this region. The columns had simple capitals (tops) and no bases. Eastern Greece and the islands (Ionia) followed the Ionic order. The columns were slimmer. They had capitals carved in ornamental curves called "volutes", and separate bases. There were differences too in the way the upper section was designed.

A third order, known as Corinthian (after the city of Corinth), was popular in the Hellenistic age, when a more ornamental style became fashionable.

Doric   Ionic   Corinthian

The finest buildings were temples – the houses of the gods and goddesses. They were usually rectangular, with columns along the sides as well as the front. Religious shrines were often built as a *tholos* – a circular building with a pointed roof. Square halls with columns inside to support the roof were built for public meetings. A long building called a *stoa* – a colonnade with a back wall – was often built around a market place, a gymnasium or the area of a religious sanctuary containing temples or shrines.

The architect Pythios inspects work on the Mausoleum (tomb) at Halicarnassus. It was built about 350, and became one of the Seven Wonders of the Ancient World.

SCULPTURE

Most of the works of art of ancient Greece vanished long ago. Sculpture has survived better than paintings, but even so the Greek sculpture in the world's museums today is only a tiny fraction of what once existed. Although we know the names of the great sculptors of Classical Athens, and we even know the names of their most famous works, we have almost no actual examples.

The Greeks' favourite material for statues was bronze, but in later ages bronzes were melted down for the sake of the metal. The few that remain were saved because they were buried or lost at sea, to be found centuries later, when people understood their value. Sculpture in marble has lasted better, and we also have some marble copies of bronze statues made in Roman times.

In everything they did, the Greeks looked for the ideal – the perfect examples which could only exist in the mind. Plato tried to imagine an ideal state. Architects searched for an ideal system of design in which rules of proportion were perfect and unchanging. In sculpture too the Greeks aimed for the perfect form, in this case the human figure. The human form was also the form of the gods; it was therefore the highest subject of art.

A sculptor polishes a finished bronze figure of a man, while a slave smelts bronze in a furnace. The Greeks learned the method of casting hollow bronze statues by the "lost wax" method in the 5th century. A model is made in wax on top of a core of clay and covered with another layer of clay. It is then heated, and the melted wax drained through a hole. Molten bronze is poured into the empty space. When it hardens, the clay mould is removed.

Temples and other buildings were decorated with sculpture "in relief" – with the carved figures attached to the background.

The Greeks mastered human anatomy quite suddenly, round about the beginning of the 5th century. Statues of gods, which had earlier been stiff and unhuman, became perfectly natural and relaxed. They were no longer just symbols of gods, but real, living and breathing, godlike figures. Sculptors began to experiment with figures in action, such as athletes. Later, they began to make portaits of actual people, instead of ideal types, and in the Hellenistic age, sculpture became more varied, with all kinds of emotions and actions brilliantly carved in stone, losing some nobility perhaps, but gaining in realism.

By that time, however, the city-states were in decline, and the dignity and grandeur of Classical sculpture had been lost.

The grand sculpture of the Classical age was due mainly to two geniuses, Pheidias in Athens and Polyclitus, who came from Argos. Pheidias designed the sculpture of the Parthenon, some of which is now in the British Museum, and made the huge sculpture of the goddess which once stood inside it.

Because today we see only what remains in museums, we think of Greek statues as figures of plain stone or bronze with hollows for eyes. In fact, the Greeks used a lot of colour, and statues had eyes of coloured stones, amber or glass.

A portrait of the goddess Aphrodite carved in stone

A kouros (figure of a young man) from the Archaic age (left) and from the Classical age (right). In their search for the perfect form, Classical sculptors gained a clear understanding of the human body and the way muscles work.

PAINTING AND POTTERY

The Greeks liked paintings just as much as sculpture. In fact, the man who coloured a sculpture was considered as important an artist as the sculptor himself. Apart from stone, painters usually made their pictures on wooden panels.

Sad to say, not one painting from Classical Greece has survived. The only records we have of Greek painting are written descriptions. (The artist Zeuxis, it was said, painted a bunch of grapes so realistically that birds pecked at them!)

Although we have no actual paintings from Classical Greece, we do have a great deal of painted pottery. Most pottery was simply household china, but it was painted with scenes from Greek myths or scenes from everyday life (very useful to historians). The Greeks did not think of these pottery pictures as great art, but to us they are often both interesting and beautiful.

Painting the picture on a vessel before it is fired.

A potter shaping a vessel on a wheel, which is turned by a boy, probably his son.

The Greeks made pots, jars and other vessels in many different shapes. They were often painted with scenes from mythology.

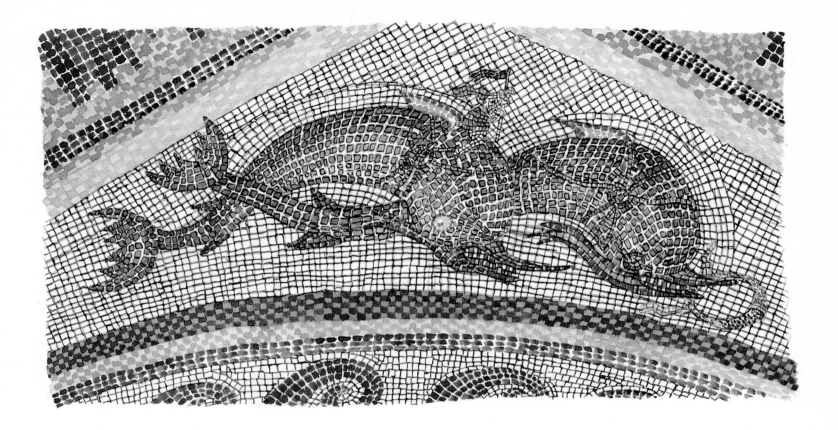

Mosaics in the Hellenistic age were made with such skill that the lines between the separate cubes of stone were almost invisible.

Pottery was made all over Greece, but Athens was the biggest producer. Attic (Athenian) pottery was exported all over the Greek world. The Athenian potter first shaped the wet clay on a wheel, which was turned by his assistant. When finished, the vessel was kept for a few days in a damp room. It was painted sometimes by the potter but often by another craftsman, and then "fired" (baked hard) in a kiln or oven.

One other kind of picture has sometimes survived – mosaic. By about 400 the Greeks were making floors of mosaic, forming patterns or pictures from black and white pebbles. By the 3rd century this simple craft had become a fine art. Mosaics were made of cubes of coloured stone, later glass, which were so realistic they looked like a painting. The surface of the cubes was tiny, sometimes as little as 1 mm across, and clever effects of colour were gained by mixing the coloured cubes in the same way as a painter puts two tiny blobs of different colours close together to make a third colour.

The Greeks were also expert metalworkers, especially in gold and silver. All the techniques used by a modern goldsmith were known to them, although they did not have mechanical tools. Greek craftsmen made small ornamental bronzes, sometimes gilded (coated with gold), carved gems and seals, which were used like a signature on documents.

The Greeks' sense of style, and their constant search for the "ideal" form, made even the most ordinary objects, such as coins or cooking pots, into what – to our eyes – are works of art.

THE GREEKS AT WAR

A giant rock-throwing catapult

Swords and shield

Spear points

Body armour

Warship's ram

A war chariot

Hand-to-hand fighting

A Hellenistic flame thrower

Sword and dagger

Hoplite's helmet

An archer

A battering ram

ARMIES

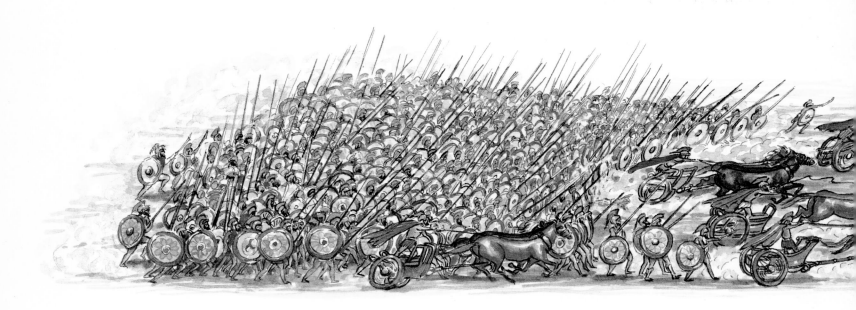

The *hoplites,* or foot soldiers, of the Greek city-states were its citizens. As wars between the states were frequent, few men lived a lifetime without having to fight at some time against somebody.

The Greeks, as long as they remained independent, never formed a united country. They were happy with the city-state, which they thought was a better form of state than any other. The only time they were united was to fight against the invasion of their powerful enemy to the east, the Persian empire, early in the 5th century.

Greek armies usually fought a pitched battle as a phalanx – a block of heavy infantry about eight lines deep, which tried to overpower the enemy by sheer force. Their weapons were spears (for stabbing, not throwing) and short swords, and they carried a large shield. They wore bronze helmets which also covered the nose and cheeks. The helmet had a crest or plume, though the plume could be removed before a fight, and the helmet could be pushed to the back of the head when not fighting. A cuirass, a tunic of metal strips with leather back, protected the body. Shin-guards called greaves were clipped on to the lower leg.

The infantry was supported by archers, who were sometimes specialists hired from Crete, and by cavalry, but both played only a small part in Greek warfare. The mountainous countryside of Greece is not suitable for cavalry movements. For the same reason, chariots were more useful as transport than in battle.

The Greeks were fierce fighters, for courage in battle was an important virtue, but

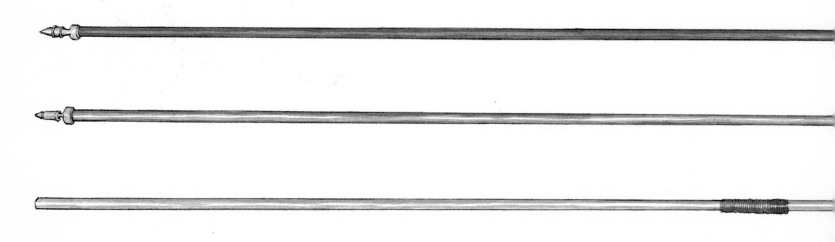

The Spartan phalanx goes into battle.

they were not great generals. Battles were confused, with a lot of shouting and muddle over orders. At the battle of Marathon (490), when the Athenians defeated a bigger Persian force, they allowed the enemy to advance against their centre and then attacked them on the flanks, but that seems to have happened by accident, not as the result of a clever plan.

Sparta was the most military state, and the Spartan army was much the biggest and the best. The Spartans, who did not have to worry about sowing seed or gathering the harvest, trained in peace time, and they were as well drilled as a professional army. But infantry, however good, cannot capture walled cities. Nor can it defeat fleets at sea. Wars in ancient Greece were not often decided by victories in pitched battles, however glorious.

Archers could fire an arrow 150 metres or so. They wore no armour and kept well clear of the main battle.

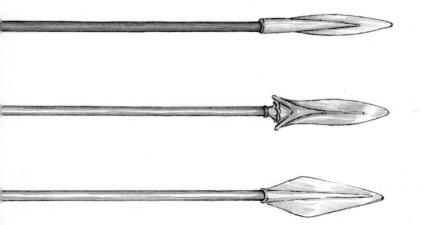

Spears for throwing and stabbing

NAVIES

While Sparta had the most powerful army in Greece, Athens commanded the sea. Before the 5th century, sea battles had been fought much like land battles. The plan was to get close to the enemy, ram her, then board her and fight like soldiers. During the Persian wars, Athens developed new tactics in naval warfare.

Greek warships, such as the trireme, were driven by oars. The oarsmen, about 200 for each ship, became soldiers when they closed with the enemy, and the early triremes had a deck which acted as a platform for the fight. The only weapon of the ship herself was a ram, a kind of spike reinforced with metal, at the bow for crashing into enemy ships. Oared ships are naturally long and thin. Too great a length made them both weaker and easier to ram. The oars of a trireme were therefore arranged in three rows one above the other. That gave them greater strength and more speed for less length.

The great victory of the Greeks over the Persian fleet at Salamis (480) was won by skilful tactics. The Persian fleet was larger, and their ships were quicker and nimbler, but the Greeks lined up their ships across the entrance to a narrow strait, protected by the rocky coast on both sides. The Persians could

not bring enough force against the concentrated Greek formation. They fell into disorder and suffered heavy losses.

It was the Greeks who learned most from this victory. They made their ships lighter and faster, and instead of simply driving straight at the enemy ships, they worked out movements by which they could disable them by breaking their oars.

The Athenians, who were natural seamen, not only had the biggest fleet, they also developed the most skilful tactics. Phormio, a commander in the Peloponnesian War, was able to pin the enemy into a circle at the battle of Naupactus by the better sailing powers of the Athenian ships. The enemy became more and more crowded, they began to bump into each other, and when they were in a real muddle, Phormio attacked.

Triremes had some drawbacks. Because they were shallow, they were in danger from the sudden storms which blow up in the Mediterranean. They had no space for sleeping or cooking, so they could never sail far from base. They could not, therefore, blockade a coast, as an army could blockade a city. As wars were often won by starving the enemy into surrender, that was a serious disadvantage.

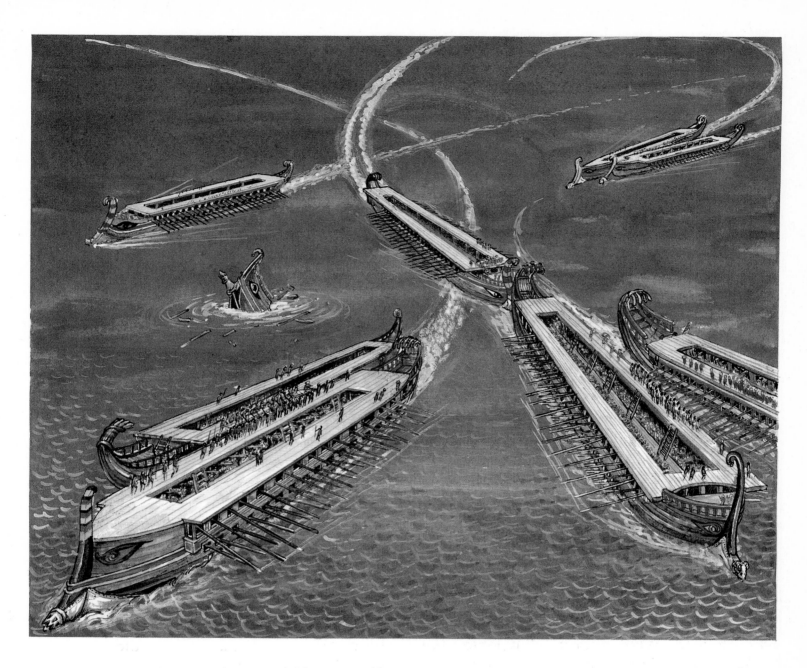

Left: *A warship under sail. Sails were useful for cruising, like the overdrive on a modern car. In a battle the sail was lowered, and the ship's movements were controlled by oars.*

Above: *In a sea battle, fighting was often hand-to-hand, the same as on land. Athenian captains tried to smash the oars of an enemy ship, which made it helpless.*

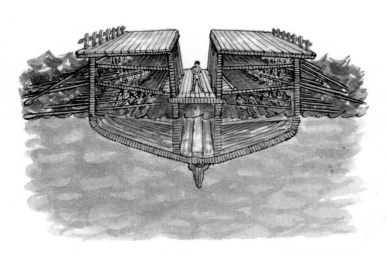

Cross-section of a Greek trireme

The warship's only weapon was its ram.

THE PELOPONNESIAN WAR

The success of Athens against the Persians made her stronger and prouder. The league of city-states which she led included most of Greece, including Ionia, but not the Peloponnese, most of which was ruled by Sparta and her allies. Because Athens was far the most powerful member, the league that had begun as an agreement between equals soon turned into an Athenian empire. Athenian laws had to be obeyed by all, and no city was allowed to leave the league.

Cities that were unhappy with Athenian rule looked for help outside the league, and the place they looked for it was Athens' great rival, Sparta. The Spartans and their allies in the Peloponnese, who were also worried by the power of Athens, were ready to help. The great war, known as the Peloponnesian War, broke out in 431.

The war was mainly a simple struggle for power: who should be the chief power in Greece, Athens or Sparta? It was also, for the Greeks, almost a "world war", because nearly every state in the region was involved. And it was also a war between two very different sorts of society: Athenian democracy (government by the people), and Spartan oligarchy (rule by a few).

The Athenian expedition to Sicily was completely destroyed, a blow from which Athens never completely recovered.

Fortified cities were hard to capture without guns, but moving towers and giant catapults were among the weapons that were used.

With one short interval, the war lasted for 27 years. The main reason why it lasted so long was that neither side was capable of defeating the other. The Spartans, a powerful land force, invaded and laid waste the land of Attica, but they could not stop Athens getting supplies by sea. The Athenians, a naval power, could not defeat the Spartans on land.

The war came to an end after the defeat of Athens's daring (or foolish) invasion of Sicily, which was an important supplier of corn to the Peloponnese. With Persian help, the Spartans were at last able to cut Athens's grain supplies from south Russia, and the Athenians were forced to surrender.

Like most wars, the Peloponnesian War solved no problems. In less than ten years, war broke out again in Greece, this time against Spartan rule, and Athens began to recover from her defeat. However, looking back, the Peloponnesian War seems to mark the end of an age.

In the years before it began, Classical Athens was at her height. The great Pericles was the leading politician, Socrates was teaching, Euripides was writing his tragedies, the Parthenon was being built. Athens was never quite so brilliant again, and the days of the city-state, the form of government that had allowed Greek civilization to develop, were drawing to an end.

THE EMPIRE OF ALEXANDER

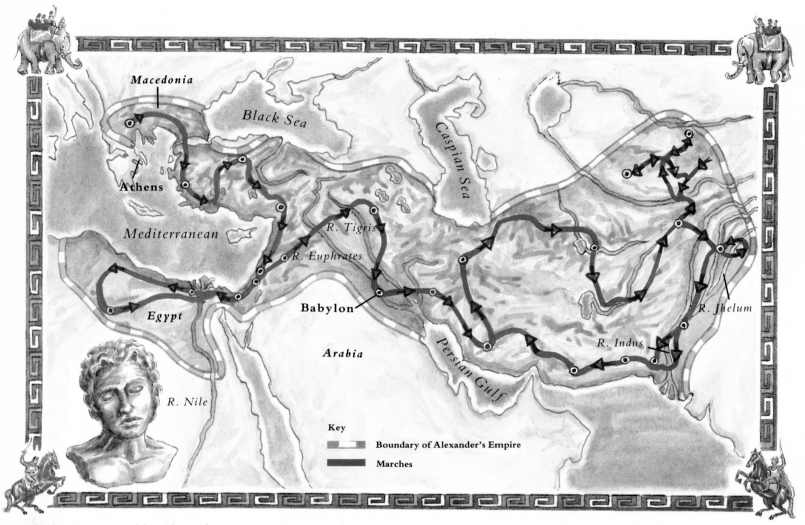

The lands conquered by Alexander.

For about fifty years, the wars inside Greece went on. First, Sparta was the greatest power. Then Thebes formed a strong league of cities in central Greece. Athens regained some of her naval strength. But, by about 350, all these powers had crumbled away. A powerful new force entered the Greek arena – Macedonia.

Macedonia was a country to the north of Greece. It was a kingdom, made up of a mixture of tribes, some of whom spoke Greek. The Greeks thought of the Macedonians as not quite barbarians, but not Greeks either. In 359 Macedonia gained an able king, Philip II, who set out to make it the greatest power in the region.

Gradually, the Greek city-states were sucked into Philip's empire. Athens held out longest, but in 338 she and her allies were defeated, and the remarkable age of the city-state came to an end.

Philip's son Alexander had even greater ambitions. At the head of a Greek and Macedonian army, he attacked the great Persian empire, and defeated it. He did not stop there. For ten years his unbeatable armies swept through the Middle East and into north-western India. By the time of his death in 323, when he was still only 33 years old, his empire covered most of the ancient civilized world.

52

After his death, Alexander's empire broke up into a number of different states. There was a great deal of fighting and confusion. The really important result of Alexander's conquests was not political but cultural. Greek, or Hellenistic, civilization spread over the whole region, from North Africa to India. Alexander himself founded 60 or 70 new cities, every one named after himself, from Egypt to Afghanistan. They were built in the Greek manner, with Greek temples, Greek houses, Greek customs and Greek government. The civilization that had begun in one small country became the civilization of the world.

In the last two centuries B.C., a new power was rising in the Mediterranean. The city of Rome was extending its rule over the whole of Italy, including the Greek colonies in the south. Soon it controlled not only Greece herself, but most of the lands that Alexander had conquered. But, unlike Alexander,

Roman rule also spread to western Europe, reaching as far as the cold, remote islands of Britain.

The Romans were already admirers of Greek culture. They read Greek literature. They copied Greek art and architecture. They took up Greek customs and ideas. They even merged their own gods with the gods of ancient Greece. Through them, the Greek tradition was passed down to the future nations of Europe.

In one of Alexander's greatest battles, near the river Jhelum in modern Pakistan, he defeated the rajah Porus, whose army contained 200 trained elephants.

MYTH AND RELIGION

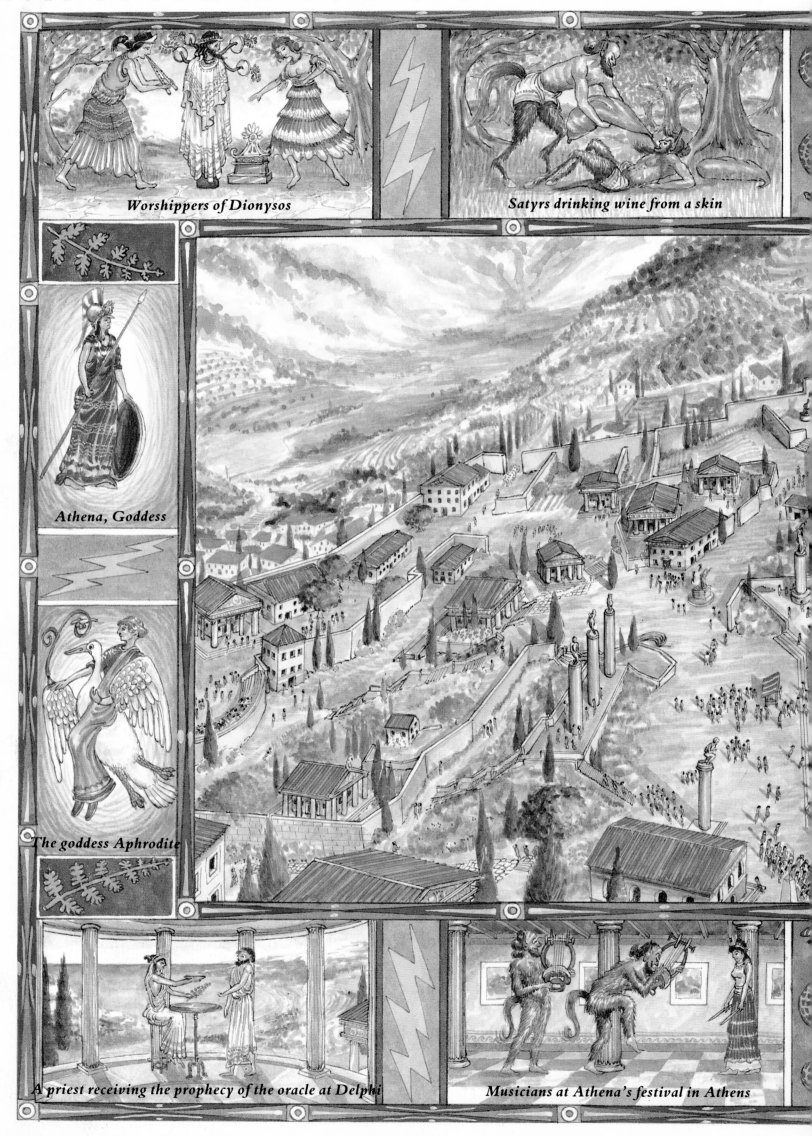

Worshippers of Dionysos

Satyrs drinking wine from a skin

Athena, Goddess

The goddess Aphrodite

A priest receiving the prophecy of the oracle at Delphi

Musicians at Athena's festival in Athens

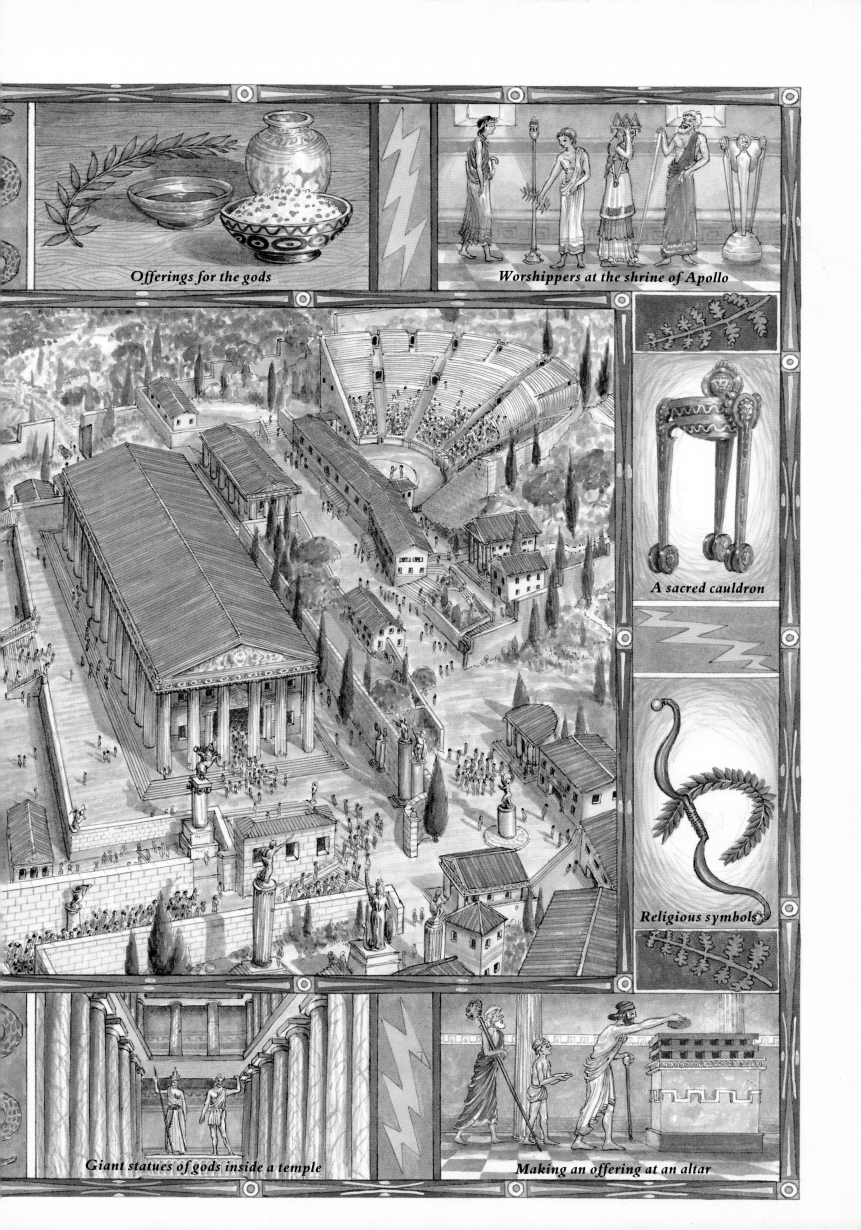

Offerings for the gods

Worshippers at the shrine of Apollo

A sacred cauldron

Religious symbols

Giant statues of gods inside a temple

Making an offering at an altar

GODS AND GODDESSES

Thunder and lightning were caused when Zeus hurled his spear.

The Greeks saw Apollo as a handsome young man.

Greek religion was not like modern religions, and it was especially unlike Christianity. To begin with, there was not one god, but many, a bewildering number.

The most important gods were the "Olympian family", who were supposed to live on the top of Mount Olympus, Greece's highest mountain. Here reigned Zeus, the father of the gods and of men, king of the Earth and Sky. The other Olympians were mostly related to him. Hera, goddess of women, was his wife; Apollo, god of music, and Artemis, goddess of hunting, were his children. Zeus also had two brothers, Poseidon, god of the Sea, and grim Hades, god of the Underworld.

The gods never died, and they had superhuman powers – for example, they could turn themselves into an animal. But in other ways, the gods were like human beings. They had human form, and human feelings. They had quarrels and love affairs. They might lose their temper, or get drunk, or behave badly. They enjoyed human pleasures too, like eating and drinking, works of art, or athletics. These activities were therefore part of the worship of the gods at religious festivals.

Inside the Parthenon in Athens was a gigantic statue of the goddess Athena, made of gold and ivory.

Unlike the gods of Christianity or Islam, the Greek gods did not stand for what was right or just. They were neither "good" nor "bad". Sometimes they might punish a person who did wrong, but that was not part of their nature. If someone wanted the help of a god in some task, he tried to get it by offering that god a sacrifice.

Although the Olympian gods and goddesses were worshipped all over Greece, some had special links with certain places. Athena, the warlike goddess of wisdom, was the patron goddess of Athens, Artemis of Ephesus. But both goddesses were also worshipped in other cities.

The temples which the Greeks built were the houses of the gods. They were not churches where people worshipped. Worship took place out of doors, and the most important part of worship was making offerings in the form of food. An animal was slaughtered at an altar, then cut up and cooked. Athena usually received an ox, while Artemis and Aphrodite preferred goats.

Fortunately, they did not mind the innards and fatty parts. The best meat was eaten by the worshippers.

The Greeks did not believe that the gods had complete control of human beings, but they did believe the gods could influence future events. A sensible man going on a voyage prayed to Poseidon, and promised an offering on his safe return.

Aphrodite, goddess of love, riding a goose. This drawing is taken from a drinking cup.

HEROES

It was sometimes possible to learn the will of the gods in advance. Omens or signs, such as a dream or an unusual happening (like an eclipse), were thought to have a meaning. Priests or professional diviners explained what they meant. They could tell a man if a business venture was likely to be a success by examining the liver of a slaughtered animal.

Oracles also foretold the future. The most famous one was the oracle of Apollo at Delphi. She was a woman called the Pythia, whose mumblings were turned into words, spoken in verse, by priests. The meaning, however, was often unclear. The oracle foretold that the Athenian invasion of Sicily would be a success, whereas it turned out to be a disaster. Afterwards, the priests explained that the oracle had not meant the Italian island of Sicily but some tiny place of the same name in Greece!

Besides the Olympian family, there were hundreds of other, lesser gods and goddesses. Household gods protected the family, in the same way as greater gods protected cities, and everything in the countryside – rivers, trees, rocks – was a spirit of some kind. Non-human creatures like centaurs, which had the head and arms of a man and the body of a horse, or nymphs, young female creatures who lived in woods and streams, also lived there. It's hard to know how seriously people believed in them.

The Greeks had many legends about heroes of the past, which are really folk tales rather than religious beliefs. Most of them were probably based on some long-forgotten real person or event.

The oracle at Apollo's shrine in Delphi gave advice to those who consulted her through the priests who controlled the shrine.

The hero Achilles, who fought in the Trojan War, died from a wound in the heel: the only part of his body that could be harmed.

The most popular hero was Heracles (the Roman Hercules), who was given twelve impossible tasks to perform ("The Labours of Hercules") and, of course, completed them all. The greatest exploit of Perseus was killing the Gorgon, who had snakes for hair and turned all who looked at her into stone. The Athenian hero Theseus killed the Minotaur, a monster who lived in a labyrinth in Crete and ate boys and girls.

The colourful patchwork of Greek mythology, with its gods and goddesses, heroes and monsters, is full of excitement, humour and adventure (also cruelty and violence). It was a great inspiration to Greek writers, like the Athenian playwrights, and it has continued to be an inspiration to Western writers and artists to this day.

Perseus killed the Gorgon, Medusa, with some help from the gods.

Heracles, a kind of Greek superman, usually wore a lionskin and carried a club.

A centaur, half man half horse. They lived in the mountains and forests and fed on raw flesh.

FINDING OUT ABOUT THE GREEKS

A papyrus document. The Greek paper was made from papyrus reeds that were split, flattened, and pressed into sheets.

Our best source of knowledge about ancient Greece is what the Greeks themselves have to tell us. They were a highly literate people and wrote things down – laws, court cases, speeches, as well as books about every subject that interested them. Of course, most of these documents disappeared long ago, and those that survive are seldom the original documents (unless they were engraved in stone) but copies of them made at some later time.

It is sad to think of how much is lost. But instead of grumbling about that, we should be thankful that so much has survived. For instance, we have most of the main works of Aristotle. From the great writers of dramatic tragedy, we have seven complete plays by Aeschylus, seven by Sophocles and no less than 19 by Euripides. That is not a lot out of the 300 Classical tragedies that still existed in Hellenistic times, but it is enough for scholars to understand quite well what Greek tragedy was like, although we have to guess at the music and dancing that were also part of the performance.

Besides documents, the Greeks left plenty of other evidence. We have seen how much we can learn about everyday life by studying the pictures painted on pottery. In the past 100 years or so, the work of archaeologists has increased our knowledge of ancient

Archaeologists skilfully piece together pieces of pottery to show the beauty of the vessels.

The remains of vanished civilizations are sometimes found buried in layers in the earth. The lower the layer, the older the object.

Greece by an enormous amount. Just as historians, being experts in the study of old documents, can learn more from them than a person with no historical training, archaeologists can discover all sorts of information from clues provided by objects that would mean nothing at all to the rest of us.

One example of how knowledge advances is provided by the Greek warship, the trireme. Until a few years ago, no one was sure what it looked like or how it sailed. Did it have three banks of oars, or one bank with three oarsmen to each oar? Learned people argued at length about such questions. Their discussions were helped by new discoveries, such as the wall painting of a 3rd-century trireme in a tomb in the ancient Greek colony of Nymphaion, in south Russia. By the 1980s, knowledge had advanced so far that it was possible to *build* a trireme, which sailed proudly in the Aegean – the first such vessel seen there for 2,000 years.

Besides books like this one, the best place to learn about ancient Greece is Greece itself. Some Classical buildings are still standing, and the museums are full of interesting objects. Museums in other countries also have objects and displays from ancient Greece. One of the best is the British Museum in London.

Greek works of art in a modern museum

TIME CHART

All dates are B.C. A small c stands for *circa*, meaning "about".

776 First Olympic Games held (according to tradition)

c. 730 Greeks begin to colonize Sicily and southern Italy

c. 700 Black-figure pottery made in Athens
Homer's *Iliad* and *Odyssey* written down

c. 520 Red-figure pottery made in Athens

499 Ionians rebel against Persian rule

490 Athenians defeat Persians at Marathon

480 Persians invade Greece; defeated at Thermopylae and Salamis

479 Final Persian defeat at Plataea

478 Athens founds Confederation of Delos, which develops into Athenian empire

456 Death of the playwright Aeschylus

447 Building of the Parthenon begun in Athens

431 Beginning of Peloponnesian War

429 Death of the Athenian statesman Pericles

c. 425 Death of the historian Herodotus

415 Athenian expedition to Sicily

413 Athenians defeated in Sicily

c. 406 Death of the playwrights Sophocles and Euripides

404 Surrender of Athens ends Peloponnesian War

400 Death of the historian Thucydides

399 Socrates commits suicide after being condemned as an "heretic"

c. 385 Death of the comic playwright Aristophanes

c. 377 Death of the physician Hippocrates

359 Philip II becomes king of Macedonia

347 Death of the philosopher Plato

343 Aristotle becomes tutor to Alexander in Macedonia

338 Athens defeated by Philip of Macedonia

336 Philip murdered, succeeded by Alexander

334 Alexander invades Asia

329 Alexander reaches India

323 Death of Alexander

322 Death of the philosopher Aristotle

c. 320 Production of red-figure pottery in Athens ends

c. 300 The mathematician Euclid at work in Alexandria

212 Death of the inventor Archimedes

168 Rome conquers Macedonia

146 Greece under Roman domination

In 146 B.C. Greece came under the domination of Rome. The Roman armies were soon to conquer most of Europe, North Africa and the Middle East. In this way the tradition of Greece was carried all over the ancient world.

INDEX

Page numbers in *italics* refer to picture captions

DATE DUE